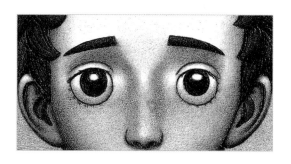

small things

small things

Mel Tregonning

ALLEN&UNWIN
SYDNEY·MELBOURNE·AUCKLAND·LONDON

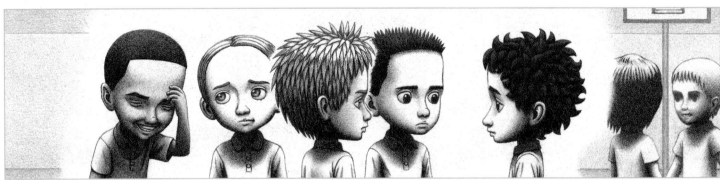

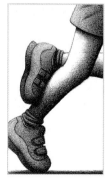

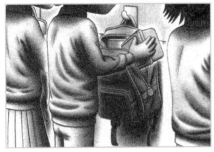

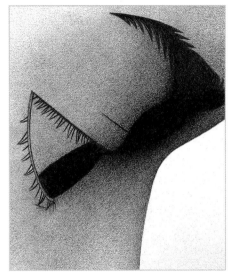
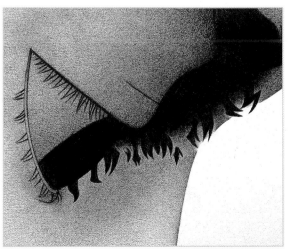

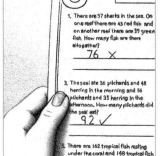

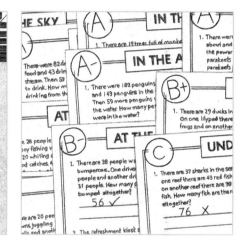

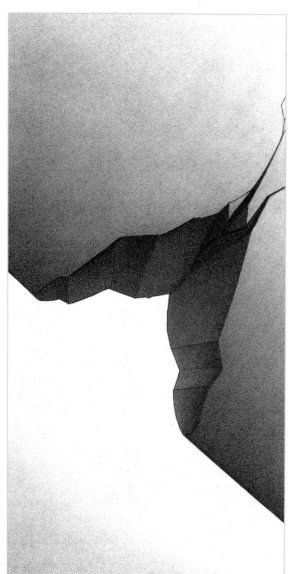

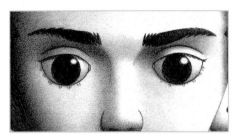

bag only holds 5 marbles
g holds 12 marbles. 99
ere bought when more
gs were sold. How many
e of bag were sold?

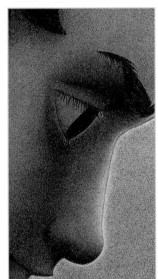

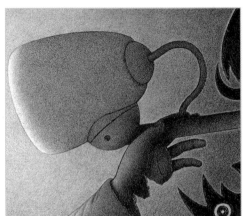

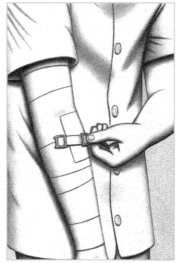
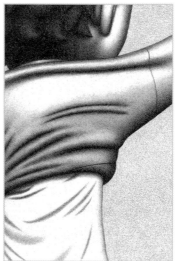

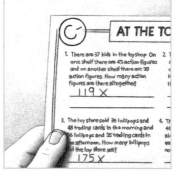

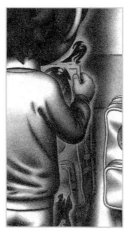

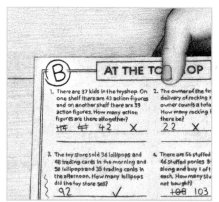

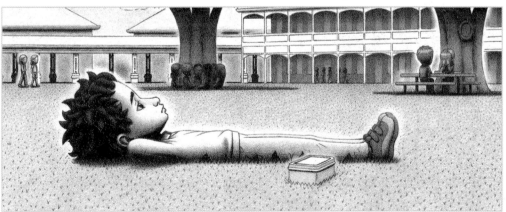

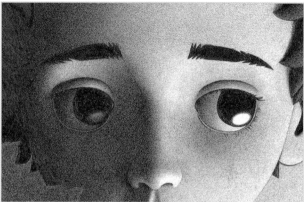

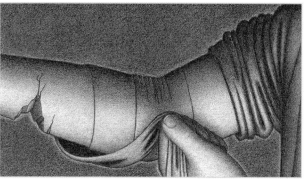

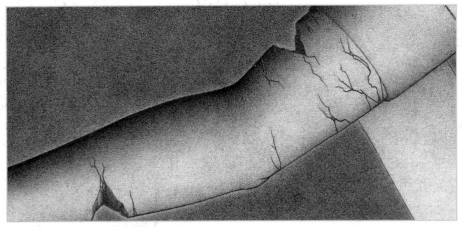

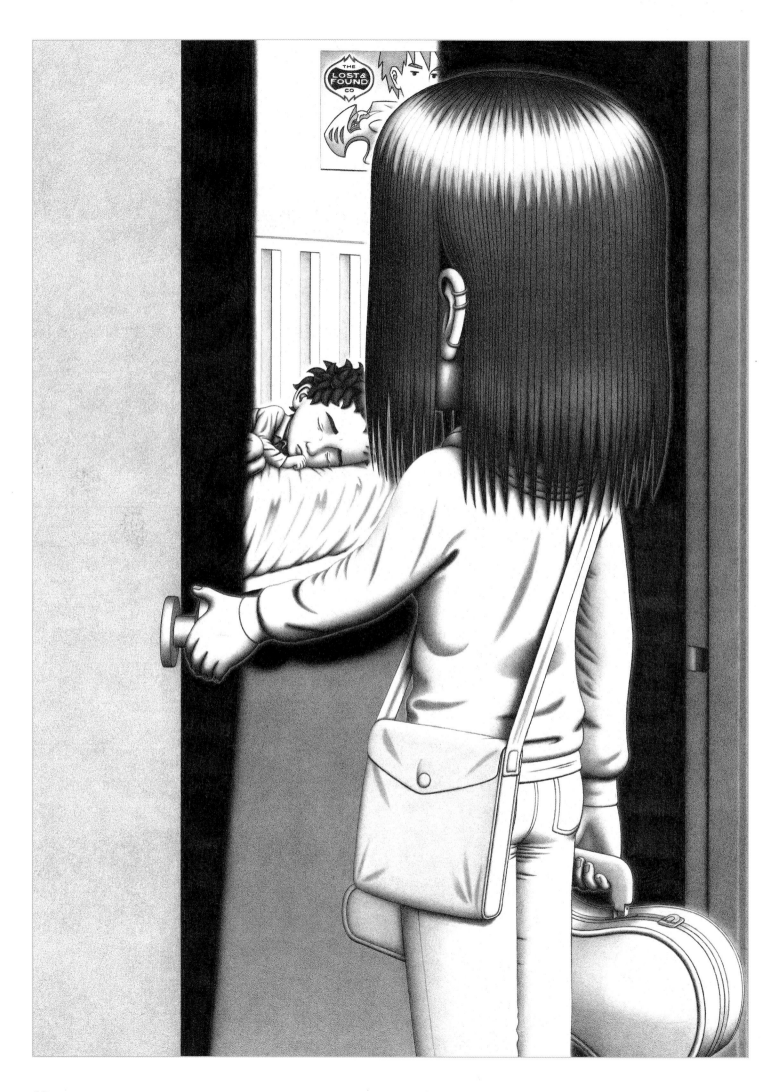

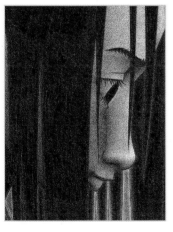

SOUTHGATE HIGH
ORCHESTRA

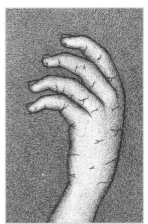
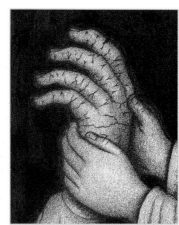

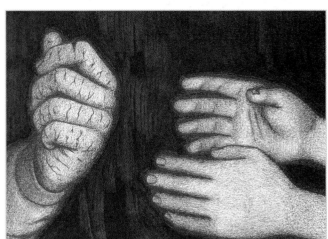

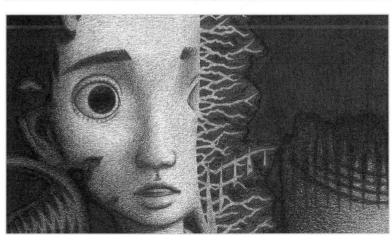

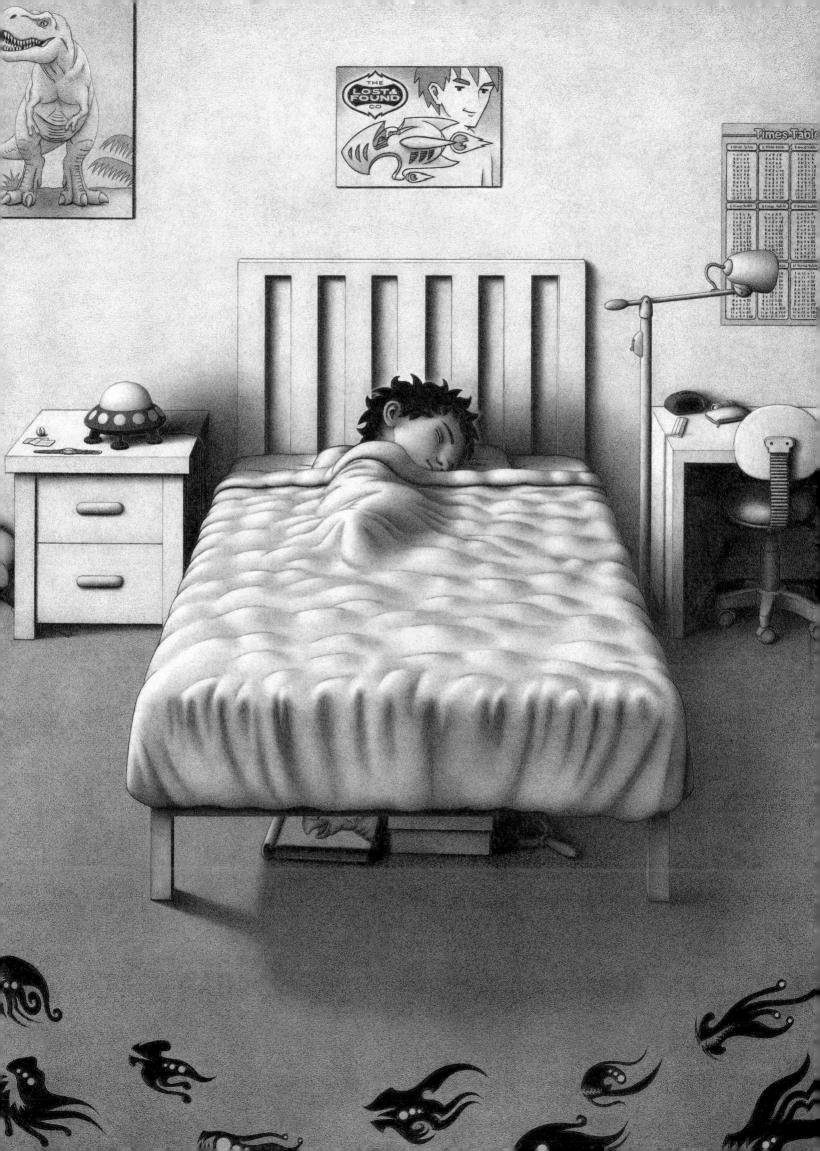

Mel,
We dedicate this book to you, we hope you can now rest.
Your dream became our dream, we have all worked so hard.
We have never loved you more and felt as proud as we do now.
Violet, Phil, Mum & Dad

First published by Allen & Unwin in 2016

Copyright © Estate of Mel R Tregonning 2016

Thanks to Shaun Tan for additional artwork direction and assistance

Allen & Unwin – Australia
83 Alexander Street, Crows Nest NSW 2065, Australia
Phone: (61 2) 8425 0100
Email: info@allenandunwin.com
Web: www.allenandunwin.com

Allen & Unwin – UK
Ormond House, 26–27 Boswell Street,
London WC1N 3JZ, UK
Phone: +44 (0) 20 8785 5995
Email: info@murdochbooks.co.uk
Web: www.murdochbooks.co.uk

A Cataloguing-in-Publication entry is available
from the National Library of Australia
www.trove.nla.gov.au.
A catalogue record for this book is available from the British Library.

ISBN (AUS) 978 1 74237 979 1
ISBN (UK) 978 1 74336 872 5

Teachers' notes available from www.allenandunwin.com

Cover and text design by Sandra Nobes
Colour reproduction by Splitting Image, Clayton, Victoria
This book was printed in March 2020 at Hang Tai Printing (Guang Dong) Ltd., China

5 7 9 10 8 6

www.meltregonning.com.au